GNOSTIC AND HISTORIC CHRISTIANITY

GERALD MASSEY

FV Editions

Contents

GNOSTIC AND HISTORIC
CHRISTIANITY

❧

My purpose in the present lectures is to enforce with further evidence, and sustain with ampler detail, the interpretation of facts, which has been already outlined in the "Natural Genesis." My contention is, that the original mythos and *gnosis* of Christianity were primarily derived from Egypt on various lines of descent, Hebrew, Persian, and Greek, Alexandrian, Essenian, and Nazarene, and that these converged in Rome, where the History was manufactured mainly from the identifiable matter of the Mythos recorded in the ancient Books of Wisdom, illustrated by Gnostic Art, and orally preserved amongst the secrets of the Mysteries.

My standpoint had not previously been taken. It

was not until this, the Era of Excavation, that we were able to dig down far enough to recover the fundamental facts that were most essential for the Student of Survivals and development to know anything certain concerning the remoter origins and evolution of the Christian System; the most ancient evidences having been neglected until now.

Instead of the Roman Church being a crucible for purging the truth from the dross of error, to give it forth pure gold, we shall have to look upon it rather as the melting-pot, in which the beautiful and noble mental coinage of Greece and Egypt was fused down and made featureless, to be run into another mould, stamped with a newer name, and reissued under a later date.

In the course of establishing Apostolic Christianity upon historical foundations, there was such a reversal of cause and outcome that the substance and the shadow had to change places, and the husk and kernel lost their natural relationship and value. All that was first in time and in originality has been put latest, in order that the prophecy might be fulfilled, and the last become first. All that preceded Christianity in the religion of knowledge, of the Gnostics, has come to be looked back upon as if it were like that representation in the German play where Adam is seen crossing the stage in the act of going to be created!

Historic Christianity has gathered in the crops that were not of its kind, but were garnered from the seed already in the soil. Whosoever tilled and sowed, it has assumed the credit, and been permitted to reap the harvest, as undisputed master of the field. It claimed, and was gradually allowed, to be the source of almost every true word and perfect work that was previously extant; and these were assigned to a personal Christ as the veritable Author and Finisher of the Faith. Every good thing was re-dated, re-warranted, declared, and guaranteed to be the blessed result of Historic Christianity, as established by Jesus and his personal disciples. It can be demonstrated that Christianity pre-existed without the Personal Christ, that it was continued by Christians who entirely rejected the historical character in the second century, and that the supposed historic portraiture in the Canonical Gospels was extant as mythical and mystical before the Gospels themselves existed. In short, the mythical theory can be proved by recovering the Mythos and the Gnosis.

The picture of the New Beginning commonly presented is Rembrandt-like in tone. The whole world around Judea lay in the shadow of outer darkness, when suddenly there was a great light seen at the centre of all, and the face of the startled universe was illuminated by an apparition of the child-Christ lying in the lap of Mary. Such was the dawn of Christianity, in which the Light of the World had come to it at last! That explanation is beautifully simple for the simple-minded; but the picture is purely ideal -- or, in sterner words, it is entirely false.

When the fountainheads of the Nile were reached at last, it was perceived that the great river did not rise from any single source in one particular place, but from a vast concourse of many tributary springs. So when we come to examine for ourselves the vast complex that passes under the vague name of Christianity, we learn that it can be traced to no one single source or locality. So far from its being an original system as product of the life, character, work, and teachings of a personal founder, we have to acknowledge sooner or later that it is more like a unique specimen of what schoolboys profanely call a "Resurrection pie."

Another popular delusion most ignorantly cherished is, that there was a golden age of *primitive Christianity*, which *followed* the preaching of the Founder and the practice of his apostles; and that there was a falling away from this paradisiacal state of primordial perfection when the Catholic Church in Rome lapsed into idolatry, Paganised and perverted the original religion, and poisoned the springs of the faith at the very fountainhead of their flowing purity. Such is the pious opinion of those orthodox Protestants who are always clamouring to *get back beyond* the Roman Church to that ideal of primitive perfection supposed to be found in the simple teachings of Jesus, and the lives of his personal followers, as recorded in the four canonical gospels and in the Acts of the Apostles. But when we do penetrate far enough into the past to see somewhat clearly through and beyond the cloud of dust that was the cause of a great obscuration in the first two centuries of our era, we find that there was no such new beginning, that the earliest days of the purest Christianity were prehistoric, and that the real golden age of knowledge and simple morality preceded, and did not follow, the Apostolic Roman Church, or the Deification of its Founder, or the humanising of the "Lamb of God," whom Lucian calls the "Impaled One of Palestine."

In an interesting book just published, entitled "Buddhism in Christendom," Mr. Lillie thinks he has found Jesus, the author of Christianity, as one of the Essenes, and a Buddhist! But there is no need of craning one's neck out of joint in looking to India, or straining in that direction at all, for the origin of

that which was Egyptian born and Gnostic bred!
Essenism was no new birth of Hindu Buddhism,
brought to Alexandria about two centuries before
our era; and Christianity, whether considered to be
mystical or historical, was not derived from
Buddhism at any time. They have some things in
common, because there is a Beyond to both. The
crucial test, however, is to be found on the thresh-
old, at the first step we take, in the doctrine of the
divine Fatherhood. The supreme *rôle* assigned to the
Christ of the Gospels, as of the Gnostics, is that of
Manifestor and Revealer of the Father in heaven.
His sign-manual is the seal of the Father. A dozen
times, according to Matthew, he calls God, "My
Father." In John's Gospel, he says, "I and my Father
are one." "I am come in my Father's name." "My
Father hath sent me." "My Father hath taught me." "I
am in my Father." "The word ye hear is my Father's."
Buddha makes no revelation of the mythology. The
Buddha is the veiled God unveiled, the un-mani-
fested made manifest, Buddha, like Putha (or
Khepr-Ptah), was begotten by his own becoming,
before the time of the divine paternity. There being
no real Father-God in Buddhism, the Buddha has
none to make known on earth. The doctrine was
Egyptian, as when it is proclaimed in the Texts that
Horus is "the son who proceeds from his father,"

and Osiris is the "father who proceeds from his son."

Again, in the Hindu myth of the ascent and transfiguration on the Mount, the Six Glories of the Buddha's head are represented as shining out with a brilliance that was blinding to mortal sight. These Six Glories are equivalent to the six manifestations of the Moon-God in the six Upper Signs, or, as it was set forth, in the Lunar Mount. During six months, the Horus, or Buddha, as Lord of Light in the Moon, did battle with the Powers of Darkness by night, whilst the Sun itself was fighting his way through the Six Lower Signs. Now, in the Gospel according to John, there is no contest with Satan, and no Transfiguration on the Mount! Instead, we have the "Light of the world," which is in heaven, warring with the Darkness, and manifesting His glory in six miracles -- no more, no less -- answering the Six Glories of the Buddha's head on the Mount, or the six manifestations in the luminous hemisphere of the superior signs. The "beginning of his signs," by which Jesus "manifested his glory," was the turning of water into wine. The sixth, and last, of these, was the raising of Lazarus, which corresponds exactly with the rising of the Mummy-constellation (Sahu) of Orion, which ascended as the star of the Resurrection, when the solar god returned from the dark hemisphere of the underworld, or the sun re-entered the sign of the Bull at the vernal equinox. The source of all is the identifiable astronomical allegory in the Soli-Lunar phase, but the fable followed in the Gospel is Egyptian, not Buddhist. The Christ is one with Horus as Lord of the Lunar light, who manifested the glory (or the Six Glories) of his father, in the six upper signs, as his only-begotten Son. The claim now made is that the common Mythos determined the number of the six Glories, or six Miracles, and the history was moulded accordingly.

I also think that Jesus -- or Joshua-ben-Pandira -- *was* an Essene. That is, he was a Nazarite, and the Nazarites were one with the Essenes. And these, for example, are amongst the "sayings" in the Book of the Nazarenes. "Blessed are the peacemakers, the just, and 'faithful.'" "Feed the hungry; give drink to the thirsty; clothe the naked." "When thou makest a gift, seek no witness whereof, to mar thy bounty. Let thy right hand be ignorant of the gifts of thy left." Such were common to all the Gnostic Scriptures, going back to the Egyptian. This is a Nazarene saying from the Book of Adam:--"No poor sculpture of earth has fashioned his throne. The palace of the King was not built up by earthly masons." And this is from an Egyptian hymn:--"He is not graven in marble, nor adored in sanctuaries. There is no building that can contain him." In the ancient Egyptian "Maxims of Ani" we read:--"The sanctuary of God abhors noisy demonstrations. Pray humbly with a loving heart, all the words of which are uttered in secret. He will listen to thy words; He will accept thy offerings. Exaggerate not the liturgical prescriptions; it is forbidden to offer more than is prescribed. Thou shalt make adorations in his name." These contain the essence of the early verses in the 6th chapter of Matthew, where the injunctions given are:--"Sound not a trumpet before thee, etc. Pray in secret to thy Father, which is in secret, and he shall recompense thee. And in praying use not vain repetitions." Ani denotes one of the names of Taht who, as Mati = Matthew, wrote down the Sayings of the Lord, some of which are amongst these Maxims.

But, unfortunately, you cannot prove anything, or, still more unfortunately, you *can* prove anything from the Gospels! You must first catch your Jesus, before you pretend to tell us what he was personally, and what were his own individual teachings. These "sayings of mine," cannot be judged as *his* if they were pre-extant, and can be proved to be anyone's sayings, or may be identified as ancient sayings, whether Buddhist, Nazarene, Apocryphal, or Egyptian. Also, there are different versions of the same sayings in the Gospels! In Matthew, we read: "Blessed are they that hunger and thirst after righteousness." In Luke it is:--"Blessed are ye that hunger now." In Matthew:--"Blessed are the poor in spirit." In Luke:--"Blessed be ye poor. Woe unto you that are rich!" Which, then, is the version that is personal to Jesus, the Nazarene? or where is the sense of claiming that the personal Jesus was an Essene or Nazarite -- one of those who never touched wine, or strong drink -- when one of the inspired writers testifies that he was described as a glutton, and a wine-bibber; and, according to another, his very first miracle was the turning of water into wine for a marriage feast? Suppose we admit that you have laid hold of Joshua, the Essene, the Nazarite, the reputed Great Healer, the Comforter, what can you make of a character so inhuman as this?

A poor Canaanitish woman comes to him from a long distance and beseeches him to cure her daughter who is grievously obsessed. "Have mercy on me, O Lord," she pleads. But he answered her not a word. The disciples, brutes as they were, if the scene were real, besought him to send her away because she cried after them. Jesus answered, and said:--"I was only sent to the lost sheep of the House of Israel." She worships him, and he calls her one of the dogs. And it is only her extreme deference that wins a kindly word from him at last. The Essenes and Gnostics absolutely denied the physical resurrection, because they were Spiritualists; therefore, it was impossible for an Essene to have taught the resurrection of the dead at the Last Day as Jesus is made to do. (John vi. 39, 40, and xi. 24.)

Again, if the pupil of Ben Perachia was an Essene, or, as reputed, an initiate in Egyptian mysteries, he never could have endorsed the mistakes attributed to Moses; never would have died for the reality of a parable, which he must have known to be astronomical. As one of the Magi or an Essene, he would understand the "Doctrine of Angels," *i.e.*, of the cycles of time, the character of the Kronian Messiah and the Coming in 400 years, according to the prophecy of Esdras. He would know the celestial nature of the Seventy-two whose names were written in Heaven as servants of the Lord of Light, and who had been with him "from the beginning" as the opponents of the Seventy-two *Sami* who served Sut-Typhon, the devil of darkness. He would know that the myths were not to be fulfilled in human history, and could not have personally set up the crazy claim that he was the messenger of Hebrew prophecy in person. No. The claims are made in his name by those who naturalized the Mythos on its Hebrew-Aramaic line of descent in Matthew,

Egyptian in Luke, and Greek in John. What we do hear is not the voice of the founder teaching one thing at one time and the direct opposite at another; we hear the voices of the different sections, each proclaiming its own particular doctrines and dogmas, each assigning them to the Christ as their typical teacher, in the course of making out a personal history from the Mythos, and of giving vent to their own particular prejudices.

The sayings of the Lord were prehistoric, as the sayings of David (who was an earlier Christ), the sayings of Horus the Lord, of Elijah the Lord, of Mana the Lord, of Christ the Lord, as the divine directions conveyed by the ancient teachings. As the "Sayings of the Lord" they were collected in Aramaic to become the *nuclei* of the earliest Christian gospel according to Matthew. So says Papias. At a later date they were put forth as the original revelation of a personal teacher, and were made the foundation of the historical fiction concocted in the four gospels that were canonized at last. In proving that Joshua or Jesus was an Essene there would be no more rest here than anywhere else for the sole of your foot upon the ground of historic fact. You could not make him to be the Founder of the Essene, Nazarite or Gnostic Brotherhoods, and communities of the genuine primitive Christians that were extant in various countries a very long while before the Era called Christian.

Nor is there any need to go to India for the original healers, called Essenes or Therapeutæ. The dawn of civilisation arose in Egypt, with healing on its wings. Egypt was the land of physicians through all her monumental history. Amongst the nations of antiquity she stands a head and shoulders above the rest; first in time and pre-eminent in attainment. Egypt was the great physician of the human race, and she sent out her medical missionaries from the earliest times. The Essenes were the same as the Therapeutæ or Healers, and they are the healers by name in Egyptian. Philo farther identifies their name with Essa in Hebrew, for healing. But Egypt had given birth to the Essenic name, and, therefore, to the persons named, before the letter E existed; that was previous to the middle empire (which ended over 4,000 years ago). In old Egyptian, the word Usha means to doctor. Whence the Ushai, later, Eshai, or Essenes, are the healers and physicians Josephus has compared the Pythagoreans with the Egyptian Therapeutæ or Alexandrian Essenes; and attempts have been made to show the derivation of Buddhist doctrines from India through Pythagoras whose name has been derived from Put = Buddha and Guru, a teacher with intent to prove that he was a teacher of the religion of Buddha. But the Egyptian Putha (the original of Buddha as I suggest) is indefinitely older than any known Buddha in India; therefore, as Pythagoras was learned in the wisdom of Egypt and was a teacher of it, I should derive his name from Putha (Ptah) and Khuru (Eg.), the Voice or Word of; as a teacher of the Cult of Putha or Ptah, the Opener and "Lord of Life."

Also, when he entered the first stage of the Essenic mysteries as a student of divinity, the Initiate was presented with an axe; that is the Egyptian hieroglyphic of divinity, called the Nuter; the sign with which the name of the priest, prophet, or Holy Father, was written. Philo informs us that the Jewish lawgiver (Moses) had trained into fellowship a large number of those who bore the name of Essenes. There were both Egyptian and Jewish communities of the healers preceding those that were known by the Christian or Gnostic names. Jerome calls the Essenes or Therapeuts "The monks of the old law," and Evagrius Ponticus speaks of "A monk of great renown who belonged to a sect of the Gnostics" that dwelt near Alexandria, and were known by name as the "Christian Gnostics." Clement of Alexandria also claimed to be a Gnostic Christian. As M. Renan points out, the life of the so-called Christian hermits was first commenced in Egypt.

Ages earlier there had been Egyptian communities of recluses, both male and female, near the Serapæum of Memphis, which were supported by the State. In Philo's letter to Hephæstion, he says the cells of the Egyptian healers are scattered about the region on the farther shore of Lake Mareotis, in Egypt. Pliny speaks of the "Ages on ages" during which the Essenes had existed, and Epiphanius, about the year 400, says,--

> *"The Essenes continue in their first position, and have not changed at all."*

Such permanency, of course, demands a long period of induration. But it is enough for the present argument to know they were extant for at least 150 years before the Christian era. Epiphanius also admits that the Christians were at first called Therapeutæ and Jesseans, an equivalent name, as he explains, for the Essenes. They were all healers and doctors. As the Ushai or Jesseans they were already extant as the healers by name, independently of any personal Jesus or Joshua the Healer. Also, in Greek the verb for healing comes from the same root as the name of Jesus. The Essenes were healers, not because they were the workers of mythical miracles like Jesus, but because they were profound students of Nature's secret powers; because they were masters of the science of mental medicine, consciously able to draw on the spirit-world for healing influences!

They had discovered that health was infectious as well as disease, and that the capacity for receiving and giving, as a medium of the higher life, depended on conditions that could be cultivated in this life. Hence the stress they laid on personal purity and its eight stages of attainment. They were healers by virtue of the Christ within. Again, we learn from pseudo-Dionysius, the Areopagite, that the name of healer, *i.e.*, the "Essene" or Therapeut, whom Eusebius calls the Curate, was employed in the early Church to denote the perfected Adept, who had attained the highest standing, just as it was with the earlier Essenes. The current expression,--"A Cure of Souls," or a "Curacy," still shows the Christian line of descent from the pre-Christian healers.

We sometimes hear of early Christian Communities in which there was no private property, but all things were held in common, as we read in the Book of Acts; although in that case the Twelve would but constitute a *late* community. The members of these brotherhoods are said to have dwelt together in perfect equality; in fact, to have lived according to those principles of liberty, equality, and fraternity which were formulated as an aim of the French Revolution! But such societies *did not first originate* as the result of establishing "*Historic Christianity.*" They did not come from the Twelve Apostles, nor from the church at Jerusalem, nor from Rome. They were founded by the prehistoric Christians, who were primitive enough to practise their creed instead of merely preaching it as a faith. But such primitive Christians were quietly at work in various parts of the world, giving health to the sick, peace to the troubled, freedom to the slave, and knowledge to the ignorant, long before the existence of Papal or Apostolic Christianity.

Philo-Judæus, who was one of the Essenes -- but does not seem to have met with the Gospel Jesus amongst them, or heard of him -- Philo says of them, --"Three things regulate all they learn and do -- viz., love to God, love of virtue, love for man. A proof of the first is the matchless sanctity of their entire life, their fear of oaths and lies, and the conviction that God is only the originator of good, never of evil. They show their love of virtue by their indifference to gain, glory, and pleasure; by their temperance, perseverance, simplicity, absence of wants, humility, faithfulness, and straightforwardness. They exemplify their love for their fellow-creatures by kindness, absence of pretensions, and lastly by the community of goods." There you have what is termed an Ideal Christian Community! but this was a Reality, and it was not founded by any personal Jesus; nor was it a result of his personal teachings being reduced to practice. It preceded, and was not a birth of, Historic Christianity.

Philo tells us that those who retired from the turmoil of public life to dwell apart in solitary places (these being the precursors of the monks and nuns in the Roman Church) handed over their private property to others, and left their parents, brothers and sisters, wife and child, and gave up all to the mysteries of a dedicated life. This, which was a common reality with the Essenes, is set forth as an Ideal when the Canonical Teacher says--"If any man cometh unto me, and hateth not his own father and mother and wife and children and brethren and sisters, yea, and his own life also, he cannot be my disciple." Here the ideal is perhaps a trifle overdone. The Essenes did not express or inculcate any such spirit of hatred to all one's relations. They were no such rabid anti-naturalists as that! The peaceful Essenic spirit is not present, but rather the spirit of Christian persecution that lighted the fires of martyrdom.

Of those Essenes who moved about in the world Josephus tells us (he also was an Essene in early life who did not find Jesus), "They have no one certain city, but many of them dwell in every city; and if any of them come from other places, what they have lies open for the strangers, just as if it were their own -- for which reason they carry nothing at all with them on their travels; nor do they buy or sell anything one to another, but every one of those who have gives to him that requires it."

The Essenes were phenomenal Spiritualists, in the current sense, who walked with open sight, and could never become the blind followers of the shut-eyed faith of the Historicisers, who banned the "malignant spirit of free inquiry." As Spiritualists they could not, and did not, believe in the resurrection of the body, consequently a corporeal resurrection of the Christ was a fundamental fallacy upon which no Essene or Gnostic could found at any time. So Anti-Christian were they in the Catholic sense, and so opposed to the Messiah of pubescence, the Christ according to the flesh, that they repudiated anointing with oil, and considered it to be a filthy defilement. Therefore their Christ did not depend upon any external anointing in baptism at the age of thirty years, and they never could become Christians as the anointed ones. They were the opponents of all blood-sacrifice, animal or human. The only sacrifice upheld by them was that of the self. Therefore they did not accept the bloody sacrifice of the incarnate Son of God when it was proclaimed.

The Essenes as Gnostics held that every man must be his own Christ. Their Christ came within -- the Christ that could not become historical without. In the minds of those who knew, Historic Christianity was repudiated beforehand; and it was as impossible after the facts were forged, the falsehood established, and the dogma was founded, as it was before; consequently those Gnostics who had been Ante-Christians beforehand were of necessity Anti-Christians afterwards.

The Essenes discarded the Pentateuch and repudiated most of the later prophets -- that is, they rejected the groundwork of the future redemption of mankind, together with the Fall that never was a fact, and the fulfilment of prophecy which never could be human. The Essenes and other Gnostics are constantly charged by the ignorant Christians with turning very plain matters of fact into fantastical parables. M. Renan talks of Simon's and Philo's allegorising exegesis as if the ancient fables had been historic facts which the Gnostics perverted into myths. They were nothing of the kind. They were fables and allegories from the first -- the mysteries that were taught in parables -- and all Gnostics rejected the historic explanation from beginning to end, because they preserved the true interpretation of the supposed history. Philo tells us--"They regard the letter of each utterance as the symbol of that which was concealed from sight, but was revealed in the hidden meaning"--not by its being rationalised into history. Mythology is, in its way, as real as mathematics, but its way is not that of the literalisers, who have made the symbolism false on the face of it to the underlying natural facts.

The fall of man, the temptation of the serpent and the coming of a Messiah were not historic realities, which the Gnostics converted into their allegories. It is altogether misleading to speak of the allegorizing Essenic and Docetic methods of exegesis, as if the Gnosis consisted in whittling away and attenuating the solid facts of history! That is merely echoing the language of those who were at war with the Gnostic interpretation, on behalf of the supposed history by which we have been misled. The allegories were first; and they are final; the history had no deeper foundations. The Essenes knew the hidden nature of these representations and taught it "through symbols, with time-honoured zeal," being in possession of the books of wisdom and other scriptures than ours. They were the jealous preservers of the hidden Gnosis, and qualified expounders of the ancient mysteries by means of the secret tradition. The initiate was sworn to keep secret the scriptures of the hidden wisdom and not to communicate the Gnosis to others, not even to a new member except in the same way in which it had been communicated to him. But it was especially prescribed that the "Doctrine of the Angels," *i.e.* of the time cycles, was not to be revealed to any non-Essene. Unfortunately that secrecy in the mode of communication became the fatal curse of all the ancient knowledge by allowing the false to come first in being publicly proclaimed.

De Quincy, in his essay on the Essenes, has remarked on the monstrosity of the omission when the Christians are not even mentioned by the Jewish historian, Josephus. There is the same portentous omission when the Essenes are never mentioned in the Christian Gospels. They are there in fact, though not by name; nor as any new-born brotherhood. They are only there in disguise, because historic Christianity has drawn the mask over the features of primitive Christianity. The existence of primitive and prehistoric Christians is acknowledged in the Gospel according to Mark when John says, --"Master, we saw one casting out devils in thy name, and he followeth not us." That, as the context shows, was done in the name of the Christ, and, consequently, such were Christians.

According to the account in Matthew, before ever a disciple had gone forth or could have begun to preach historic Christianity, there was a widespread secret organization ready to receive and bound to succour those who were sent out in every city of Israel. Who, then, are these? They are called "The Worthy." That is, as with the Essenes, those who have stood the tests, proved faithful, and been found worthy. According to the canonical account these were the prehistoric Christians, whether called Essenes or Nazarenes; the worthy, the faithful, or the Brethren of the Lord. "Peace be with you!" was the greeting or password of the Essenes, and also of the Nazarenes, to judge from its appearing in the book of Adam. And in the instructions given to the Seventy (Luke x. 5) it is said:--"Into whatsoever house ye enter first say, 'Peace be to this house.'"

After the resurrection the mystic password is employed three times over by the risen Christ. And "He who comes with peace" is the name of the Egyptian God, Iu-em-hept, the son of Atum, who, as the coming son, is Iu-su = Jesus. We also learn from the Clementine Homilies (3, 19) that the "Mystery of the Scriptures" which was taught by (or ascribed to) Christ was identical with that which *from the first* had been communicated to *those who were the Worthy.* We may learn from the Gospel according to Luke that the "Worthy" were those who had been initiated into the Mysteries of the Gnosis, and who were "accounted Worthy" to attain that "resurrection from the dead" in this life, which Paul was not altogether sure about--"those who knew that they could die no more, being equal to the angels as sons of God and sons of the Resurrection." Such were then extant as prehistoric Christians (ch. xx. 35-6).

These communities of the primitive Christians had long been accustomed to send forth their bare-footed apostles into all the known world, to inculcate the common brotherhood of man, founded on the common fatherhood of God, and to labour for the family of the human race. That had been the practice in the past which was afterwards made a matter of precept in the present, and a prospect for the future! For this ancient practice of the Essenes is reduced to the precept of the teacher made personal, who says, "Go your way; carry neither purse, nor scrip, nor shoes;" and gives instructions to do the very things the Essenes had always done! The supposed personal teacher and historic founder of primitive Christianity is made to say to his follow-ers, "A new commandment I give unto you that ye love one another." But the statement is entirely untrue. There was nothing new in it! This was a primary commandment of the Essenic communities who had practised the principles they professed, and had lived for ages according to the golden rule which is afterwards laid down as a divine command, a direct revelation from God, in the Gospels.

No matter who the plagiarist may be, the teaching now held to be divine was drawn from older human sources, and palmed off under false pretensions. Josephus declares in his account of the Essenes, that "Whatever they say is firmer than an oath; but swearing is entirely avoided by them. They consider it worse than perjury." And such is the original revelation in the Gospel. But I was sorry to find, in the Clementine Homilies, that the same speaker breaks the Essenic pledge, for it is there written,-- "And Christ said (with an oath), *Verily I say unto you, unless ye be born again of the water of life, ye cannot enter in the kingdom of heaven.*" Thus we have an Essene who swears as well as tipples and plays the part of Bacchus. Again, Jesus is presented as the original revealer of the mysteries and author of the Gnosis. He says to his disciples,--"*It is given you to know the mysteries of heaven;*" but the Essenic Communities always had been composed of those who were in possession of the Gnosis, and had already obtained and sacredly preserved the knowledge of the mysteries of the kingdom of heaven, which they had taught only in parables.

The divine morality inculcated in the Sayings ascribed to Jesus had been completely forestalled by the Essenes in their lives and works, their individual characters, common practices, and societary conditions. His words are but a later echo of their very human deeds. We are told that Jesus taught mankind to pray, --"Thy kingdom come, thy will be done on earth as it is in heaven." But this was exactly what the prehistoric Christians had been working out in life. They strove to found the kingdom there and then, and realise the world to come in this. Everything noble and ennobling, unselfish and spiritual, in the ethics of Jesus, or rather in the sayings assigned to him as a teacher of men, had been anticipated by the Egyptians, the Essenes, and the primitive Christians of the Gnostic religion. Nothing new remained to be inculcated by the Gospel of the new teacher, who is merely made to repeat the old sayings with a pretentious air of supernatural authority; the result being that the true sayings of old are, of necessity, conveyed to later times in a delusive manner. The commandments are not new. Life and immortality were not brought to light by any personal Jesus, but by the Christ of the Gnosis.

The most important proclamation assigned to Jesus turned out to be false. The kingdom of God was not at hand; the world was not nearing its end;

the catastrophe foretold never occurred; the second coming was no more actual than the first; the lost sheep of Israel are not yet saved. And the supposed Divine Truth in very person remains exposed as the genuine false prophet to this day, or rather as the mere mouthpiece of the most ignorant beliefs of that day. It may be said more justly of Historic Christianity, than of anything else within the compass of my knowledge, that what is true in it was not new, and that which was new in it is not true! It is not new, because it represents the ancient Mythos under an intended disguise. It is not true, because it is not a genuine history. The supposed human original, set forth in the Gospels, is but the mundane shadow of the Gnostic Christ.

Christianity began as Gnosticism, refaced with falsehoods concerning a series of facts alleged to have been historical, but which are demonstrably mythical. By which I do not mean mythical as exaggerations or perversions of historic truth, but belonging to the pre-extant Mythos. Of course, the setting-up of this vast falsehood made all truth a blasphemy. "The Gnostics," says Irenæus, "have no gospel which is not full of blasphemy." Their crime was that they denied the Christ carnalised, and they were denounced as being Anti-Christian, because they were *Ante*-Christian!

We are told in the Book of Acts that the name of the *Christiani* was first given at Antioch; but so late as the year 200 A.D. no canonical New Testament was known at Antioch, the alleged birthplace of the Christian name. There was no special reason why "the disciples" should first have been named as Christians at Antioch, except that this was a great centre of the Gnostic Christians, who were previously identified with the teachings of the mage Simon of Samaria. Simon had taught the people of Antioch for a "long time" before, and had been accepted by them "from the least to the greatest" (Acts). Simon was the great Antichrist in the eyes of the founders of the belief in Historic Christianity, for whom the Ante-Christ was always, and everywhere, the Antichrist; and it was necessary to account for there being Christians, other, and earlier, than the believers in a carnalized Christ. This was clumsily attempted in the "Acts," by making Simon become a baptised convert to the new superstition, and then back-sliding--a common mode of accounting for Gnostic heretics, but false on the face of it.

Irenæus shall furnish us with a crucial instance of the orthodox lying on this subject. He tells us that the Gnostics, such as those who followed Valentinus and Marcion, in the second century, had no existence before these later teachers (B. III. Ch. 4, 3); whereas he had already stated in his first book, that Simon of Samaria was the first and foremost of all the founders of Gnosticism, and the father of all its heresies; and he was a century earlier. Simon had brought in the Gnosis from Alexandria. He taught his doctrines, and wrought his wonders long anterior to the apostles of the later creed. Epiphanius acknowledges that all the heretical forms of Christianity were derived from the Pagan Mythology -- that is, they were survivals of the original prehistoric Gnostic religion.

It is obvious that the Roman Church remained Gnostic at the beginning of the second century, and for some time afterwards. Marcion, the great Gnostic, did not separate from it until about the year 136 A.D. Tatian did not break with it until long after that. In each case the cause of quarrel was the same. They left the Church that was setting up the fraud of Historic Christianity. They left it as Gnostic Christians, who were anathematised as heretics, because they rejected the Christ made flesh and the new foundations of religion in a spurious Jewish history.

The Church in Jerusalem, at the head of which was James, called the "brother of the Lord," was one of the Essenic or Therapeutic communities that were founded by the Gnostic Nazarenes. James was reputed to have been a follower of Joshua, the Nazarene -- i.e., Ben Pandira -- who was converted more or less into the later Jesus of Nazareth. The Jewish legends show that he was of the Nazarene sect. But no *Nazarene* brotherhood could have been founded on any supposed Jesus of Nazareth. They also show that James was a Nazarene of the ancient ascetic type -- one of those who were set apart and consecrated from the mother's womb -- one who never shaved or cut his hair, who drank neither wine nor strong drink, nor ate of any animal food; he would not anoint himself with oil, nor wear woollen garments. Bishop Lightfoot admits that the members of the early Church at Jerusalem were Gnostics, like the other Essenes: only, for him, they were heretics. He cannot make out the hiatus, which was not then filled in with the Gospel history.

Now, whether it be called Christian or pre-Christian, the Gospel of James is good, as far as it goes. It was undoubtedly the same Gospel of the Essenes that opened the poor man's door to heaven. It teaches their doctrines in their own language, and without the Historic apparatus. It puts certain things which have been disestablished on their original foothold. In the Lord's Prayer we are taught to ask the Divine Father not to lead us, his children, into temptation. But James declares emphatically that "no man should say he is tempted of God, for God cannot be tempted with evil, and he himself tempteth no man." The Epistle of James is of supreme importance.

Eusebius, the suspected forger and falsifier, when he made his fatal admission, must have known that the Scriptures of the Essenes had been utilised as *groundwork* for the Epistles and the later Canonical history. He claims the Essenes themselves as Christians when he tells us that Philo "describes with the closest accuracy the lives of our ascetics"--that is, of the Therapeutæ. He confesses "it is highly probable that the ancient commentaries, which Philo says they have, are the very gospels and writings of the apostles, and probably some expositions of the ancient prophets, such as are contained in the Epistle to the Hebrews and many other of Paul's epistles." He might have said, including the Ebionite Epistle of James, only that was to be denounced as spurious. But it is impossible to claim the Essenic Scriptures as being identical with the Canonical records, without, at the same time, admitting their prehistoric existence, their non-historical nature, and their anti-historical testimony. They could only be the same in the time of Eusebius by the non-historical having been falsely converted into the historical. This was what had been done, and that alone will explain why the earliest scriptures, which ought to have contained the historical record, have not been preserved, but were got rid of altogether when the Council of Nice "suppressed all the devices of the heretics."

I have previously shown that the real root of the whole matter can be delved down to and identified in the mythology and mysteries of Egypt. When we see the Child-Horus emerging from the lily-lotus, or holding the forefinger to his mouth, as portrayed upon the Gnostic stones and in the Catacombs of Rome, absolutely the same as on the Egyptian monuments, we know that it is the identical divinity, no matter how it came to represent the Christian Christ. But identification is more difficult when the mythical type has passed into the more mystical phase. That is, the portraits of deities are more recognisable than the hidden doctrines and veiled features of the Gnosis. Yet, the Egyptian doctrines were as surely continued by the Gnostics and the Christians as the personal likenesses of Egyptian deities were reproduced by Gnostic Art in Rome. And by aid of the Gnosis, we can recover much that has been dislimned and made indefinite in the doctrinal stage, to be left as an unfathomable mystery! For example, the Child-Horus, with finger to mouth, wherever found, indicates the divine

Word or Logos in a particular way. He was the child of the Virgin mother alone, and always remained the child. He, therefore, was not the *True Voice*, or *Voice of Truth*, only the Imperfect Word, the Inarticulate Discourse, as Plutarch calls the first Horus.

But, just as the voice of the boy changes and becomes manly at puberty, so in his second or virile character Horus, as representative of the Father, becomes a True Voice, and is the "Word of Truth" personified! In this character he was designated Har-Makheru, *i.e.*, Horus, the "Word of Truth," from Ma, Truth; Kheru, the Word. In the Egyptian texts the Word of Horus *is* Truth; the function confided to him by the Father! He vanquishes his enemies with the Word of Truth. It is said of the Osirified deceased, He goes forth with the Word of Truth. To make the Truth by means of the Word is synonymous with the giving of life here or hereafter. In a prayer to the Pharaoh it is said, "Grant us breath by the gift which is in thee of the 'Word of Truth.'" Moreover, men conquer their sins by means of this "Word of Truth" within, the Makheru conferred on them by the Deity!

This title of Makheru, the Word of Truth, was translated the *Justified* by Dr. Birch, which M. Pierret says is "unfortunate." But there is a Christian sense in which that is a correct rendering. With the Egyptians, the Christians (*o... crhsto...*), the faithful Departed, were actually *called* by this title of Makheru or the Justified. They were those who always had been saved by the "Word-of-Truth!" in Egypt long Ages before the *Christian* Era!

Now, let us return for a moment to the Epistle of James canonised in the New Testament, and called by Luther "an Epistle of Straw," because it had not a grain of Historic Christianity in it. James was the head of the Church in Jerusalem. He was titled a brother of the Lord -- no doubt in relation to the Nazarite Brotherhood; the Lord being a typical character like Horus, Mana, or Elias, who was igno- rantly assumed by the literalizers of legends to have been a Judean peasant named Jesus or Joshua. Hence the imposition of certain family details in the Canonical Gospels, which will be traced hereafter. James is believed to have died about A.D. 60. But in the whole seven chapters of this Epistle of James, excepting an opening salutation, there is not one single sign of Historic Christianity! It recognises no Jesus of Nazareth, and it announces no salvation through the atoning blood, the death, resurrection and ascension of a personal Christ.

Nothing whatever begins with or is based on the history which was afterwards made canonical, nor on the Christ that was localized at a later stage of development. Everything is absent that was and still is essential to the physical faith. Instead, we find the exact opposite of all that was made historic in the Gospels. The doctrine of salvation is Gnostic, Essenic and Egyptian. Salvation, according to James, cometh of the "Word of Truth." Speaking of the "Father of Lights" (Lord of Lights being a title of Horus) he says:--"Of his own will begat he us with the 'Word of Truth' that we should be a kind of first fruits of his creatures." "Wherefore receive ye with meekness the implanted Word which is able to save your souls." The transaction is direct between the divine father and the human soul. The Christ within is the only saviour! The total teaching of the Epistle of James is based on this ancient Egyptian Word of Truth; the implanted Word which confers the Makheru on man, which never could be represented by an historical Christ. The "Word of Truth" as rendered by James is the best possible translation of the Egyptian "Ma-Kheru." Moreover, the context shows that the Word of Truth is the Egyptian Makheru by the exhortation, "Be ye doers of the Word," which renders good Egyptian doctrine in perfect accordance with exact Egyptian phraseology.

Just as Horus Makheru was the Word of Truth; or that which was said was fulfilled indeed, so men are re-begotten in the divine likeness by the Word of

Truth; and as livers or doers of that Word they are to be saved -- as it was taught in Egypt thousands of years previously without the Word of Truth becoming incarnate in Horus as a human person. This Word of Truth, the Christ of James and Paul, which alone was able to save, is identical with that made known aforetime, which needed not to be brought down from heaven for any personal incarnation; needed not to be brought up from the dead by any physical resurrection; needed not to be sent from over the sea, because, as was said by the Mosaic mouthpiece of Egypt's Wisdom, "that Word is in thy heart that thou mayest do it!" And this is the position reoccupied; this is the teaching re-echoed by Paul, in whose mouth the Word of Truth becomes doubly anti-historic (*cf.* Deut. xxx. 12-14, with Romans x. 6, 7).

There is also a reference to the "Word of Truth" in Paul's Epistle to Timothy, which still further identifies the Makheru. The word Ma, for that which is true, originally means to hold out straight before one. And Paul exhorts Timothy, as a workman, to hold a straight course according to the Ma-kheru, or "Word of Truth." This True Voice or Word of Truth is, I take it, that living and abiding voice which is appealed to by Papias as evidence for his Christ, who was the Lord of the Logia; and, if so, his testimony thus far does not make for, but tends to invalidate, the history. Of course, he is supposed to mean the voice of contemporaries when he decries what would be the more certain voice of written records; but that is not what he means. He prefers, in reality, the traditions of the oral wisdom, and may be claimed as another witness for the non-Historical Christ. Also, the epistle to Diognetus, supposed to have been written by Marcion, contains the same doctrine as the epistle of James. Speaking of the Gnostic Christians, he says:--"They are put to death and they come to life again," and the reason of this is that "God the Invisible hath himself from Heaven planted the truth and the holy incomprehensible Word and established him in their hearts." This epistle of James is indefinitely older than the Canonical history. James is believed to have died about the year 60 of our era, and in this, one of the earliest utterances of the Church, instead of the History, we find the divine Makheru of the Egyptian mythos in a mystical and doctrinal phase.

Instead of an original gospel based on the life, character, and teachings of his own human brother, James presents us with the translated Word-of-truth--the Horus of Egypt, and the Christ of the Gnostics, who could not become historical. This beginning, then, is doctrinal, and the doctrine, like the portrait, is Egyptian. The same mythos was visibly continued in the Gnostic phase. In the Gospels, which were being compiled at least one hundred years later, we find this same Word of Truth, which was personated by Horus-Makheru and by Iu-em-hept in Egypt some 3,000 years earlier, is now represented in a personal character as Jesus the Christ.

This Word of Truth, which is doctrinal and non-historical, according to James, is the Word of Truth made flesh according to John. Also, the Christ is the Horus continued in his two characters. Hence the Word, or Spirit of Truth, which proceedeth from the Father, is to come as the mystic Paraclete who shall testify to the reality of an historic Jesus.

These two characters, as the Sayer and Doer, constitute the double foundation of the Christ in the other Gospels. The Christ of Matthew is chiefly the Sayer. The Christ of Luke is mainly the Doer. He is mighty in deed and word! He is the Healer or Doer with the Word. "What a Word is this"! exclaim the multitude, who are amazed at the miracles. Both characters had been blended in one as Horus-Makheru, the Word of Truth, who was mythical in Egypt, and who is mythical in the teaching of James before the Word was described as being made flesh, to become an historical personage in the later

Gospel according to John. This is the fatal kind of fact that turns the canonical history into fiction, and brands the falsifiers full in the face. There is no room left here for any historic fulfilment, and no need of any personal Savior or vicarious victim. The Word of Truth is the Spirit of God, the Begetter of Souls, the Christ within, the Bringer of Immortality to Man, as it is in the teaching of Hermes, of Zarathustra, of Philo, and of Paul, as well as James; as it was in Egypt, in Chaldea, in India, in all the Mysteries, no matter where the Gnosis or Kabalah may be found. In presence of the Gnosis, here as elsewhere, there is no place, no significance, in the alleged facts of a human history, lived for us by a carnalised Christ. And yet such a history was made out, and we are now able to get a glimpse of the forgers engaged in the process of making it out!

Our Canonical Gospels are a Palimpsest, with one writing so elaborated over another that the first is almost crossed out, and the rest are thoroughly confused. Yet, the whole of them have to be seen through before the matter can be really read. By holding this Palimpsest up to the light, and looking at it long and closely, we can trace the large outline, the watermark, of the Egyptian mythos, with its virgin-mother, who was Hathor-Meri--the Madonna -- its child-Christ of 12 years, and the virile adult of 30 years, who was Horus, the anointed son of that Father in heaven whom he came to reveal. This is the earliest and most fundamental of the *nuclei*. Next we find a collection of Sayings as the nucleus of the Gospel of Matthew. These sayings were attributed to the Lord, and that Lord is supposed to have been a Judean peasant, as the original author! It is noticeable, though, that the title of the Lord is not once applied to Jesus by Matthew in the earth-life, but after the resurrection he is called the "Lord."

Now, it is well known to scholars that the Gospel according to Luke is based upon, or concocted, with suitable alterations, from an earlier "Gospel of the Lord." That is, the latest gospel according to the Gnostics, preceded the earliest of those that were made canonical. This was called the "Gospel of the Lord"--the *kurios* -- and it is commonly referred to as the gospel of Marcion, the great Gnostic. But the Lord, as known to the Gnostics, was not a character that could become historical. As Irenæus declares, according to no one gospel of the heretics could the Christ become flesh; consequently the gospel of Marcion, who was the arch-heretic and very Anti-Christ of the second century, in the sight of the incipient Catholic Church, could not have been a gospel of the Christ made historical; and we have now the means of proving that it was not. When once we know that the origins were mythical, that the Christ was mystical, and the teachings in the mysteries were typical, we shall be able to utilise the gospel of Marcion as a connecting link between the Egyptian Mythos, the epistle of the Word of Truth, and the canonical history according to Luke.

"The Lord" had been Horus by name in Egypt, and the Greek kuriou, or kurios, agrees with the Egyptian kheru, for the Word, Voice, or Logos, as in Ma-kheru (earlier, Ma-khuru). This was the Lord continued as the Gnostic manifestor, their Horus, or Christ. Marcion assigned his gospel to the Christ, in the same way that the Egyptian Ritual is ascribed to Hermes. Later on, the sayings of the Lord were also called the writings, as we see by pseudo-Dionysius, who charges the Gnostics with having falsified the Writings of the Lord.

Marcion claimed that his was the one true Gospel--the one--and he pointed to the multiplicity of the Catholic Gospels, full as they were of discrepancies, in proof that they could not be genuine. In the fourth century even, there were as many different gospels as texts. As transmitted to us by the Christian copyists, who were nothing if not historicisers, Marcion's gospel opens with the statement, that "In the fifteenth year of the reign of Tiberius

Cæsar, Pontius Pilate ruling in Judea, Jesus came down to Capernaum, a city of Galilee," or "into Judea," as reported by Irenæus.

Tertullian says,--"According to the gospel of Marcion, in the fifteenth year of Tiberius, Christ Jesus *deigned to emanate from heaven, a salutary spirit.*" But, he also says, according to this "Great Anti-Christian," the Christ was a phantom, who appeared suddenly at the synagogue of Capernaum in the likeness of a full-grown man for the purpose of protesting against the law and the prophets! It would be difficult to date the descent of a phantom Christ, and impossible to date the descent of the Gnostic Christ at all, except as Lord of the æon in relation to an astronomical period! But it is certain that the Lord or Christ of Marcion is entirely non-historical. He has no genealogy or Jewish line of descent; no earthly mother, no father, no mundane birthplace or human birth. The Gnostic nature of this Christ is further and fully corroborated by both Irenæus and Tertullian. Clearly then nothing can be made of the statement on behalf of the Canonical history. This statement in Marcion's gospel takes the place of the baptism and descent of the holy spirit in Luke's; and this same date is quoted by Luke for the time when the Word of God came to John in the wilderness, which is followed by the baptism of Jesus and the transformation into the Christ or Horus of 30 years, whose unpronounceable name contained 30 letters, according to the Gnosis.

Such a beginning is entirely unhistorical, and applicable solely to the mythical Christ, who became the virile adult, the anointed son of the father at 30 years of age. Of course Christian apologists like Irenæus and Tertullian maintained that Marcion had mutilated their version of Luke; and they managed to get rid of the "Gospel of the Lord," and to suppress the writings of Marcion in proof to save us the trouble of judging for ourselves. But that was only another Christian lie, as we have now the means of knowing. The Gnostics were not the falsifiers of the historic scriptures; it was not they who had anything to falsify! Hitherto the forgers and falsifiers have been believed, and now the accusers and accused are about to change places in the witness-box and the dock. Everywhere the Gnosis was first; the history was last. You are only asked to take this view tentatively, and then let us watch the process and see how the compilers and forgers of our Luke put in the touches by which the mythos was rationalized and the human history was added to the Gnostic "Gospel of the Lord." The "Sayings of the Lord" were first, and they were not personal. The "Gospel of the Lord" was first, and the Lord was not historical.

The Jesus of Marcion like the Jesus of Esdras, of Paul, and other Gnostics, is no Jesus of Nazareth. This title has been added by Luke. Marcion's Jesus being mythical and not historical, he has no Jewish father and mother; consequently we find the test question:--"Is not this Joseph's son?" does not appear in the "Gospel of the Lord." It has been added by Luke. Again, the statement, "there came to him his mother and brethren; and they could not get at him for the crowd" (Luke viii. 9), is not to be found in Marcion's gospel; it has been added by Luke. And for what? but to manufacture and make out that human history which was at last believed in, but which had no place in any gospel according to the Gnostics or true primitive Christians! It can be proved how passage after passage has been added to the earlier gospel, in the course of manufacturing the later history.

For example, the mourning over Jerusalem (Luke xiii. 29-35) is taken verbatim from the 2nd Esdras (i. 28-33) without acknowledgment, and the words previously uttered by the "Almighty Lord" are here assigned to Jesus as the original speaker. The account of Pilate's shedding the blood of the Galileans and mingling it with their sacrifices (Luke xiii. 1) has been added by some one so ignorant of Hebrew history, that he has ascribed to Pilate an act which was committed when Quirinus was governor, twenty-four years earlier than the alleged appearance of Jesus. Again, the anti-Nazarene, anti-Gnostic passage about the publicans being baptised with water, and the Son of Man coming eating and drinking as a glutton and a wine-bibber, has been added.

In the scene on the Mount of Transfiguration, which is purely mythical, and therefore common to Osiris, Buddha, and Zarathustra, we are witness to the forging of another historical nexus in the statement that "Moses and Elijah appeared in glory and spake of his decease which he was about to accomplish at Jerusalem" (Luke ix. 31). This passage does not appear in the "Gospel of the Lord." Nor does the statement (Luke xviii. 31-34), "And he took unto him the Twelve, and said unto them, 'Behold, we go up to Jerusalem, and all things that are written by the prophets shall be accomplished by the Son of Man.'" This mode of making out the history in the New Testament by fulfilment of prophecy found in the Old was *not* adopted by the compilers of Marcion's "Gospel of the Lord." The story of the colt and the riding into Jerusalem in triumph, to turn all the Jews out of their sacred Stock Exchange, are additions to the earlier Gospel! In the scene of the Last Supper almost the whole of the text is missing from

Marcion's Gospel. Twelve verses of Luke 22 have been added!

In Marcion's Gospel there is no distribution of the Paschal Cup amongst the disciples; no promise is given that the Apostles shall eat and drink and judge the twelve tribes of Israel in the kingdom of Christ; nor is there any appointment made with the dying thief on the Cross to meet him that day in Paradise! *These have been added.* Now, this is no mere matter of a difference in doctrine! We are witnessing the very forgery of the human foundations and the insertion of the manufactured facts upon which the history was established.

The Primitive Christiani, the so-called *heretics*, who preceded the historic Christians, were all of them spiritualists in the modern sense.

In the sight of Bishop Lightfoot the Gnostic Spiritualism was "a shadowy mysticism which loses itself in the contemplation of an unseen world." *This* he looks upon as the *false* teaching and the *heresy* of the Gnostics! He knows nothing of any *underlying* natural verities, or *phenomenal* facts; only sees a refining, a mysticising and a whittling away of the Gospel histories.

But as practical Spiritualists, the Essenes had eight stages in the evolution of perfect personal purity and the attainment of the highest spiritual powers:--

1. Purity of baptism.

2. Purity from animal desire.

3. Spiritual purity.

4. The purity of a meek and gentle spirit.

5. The purity of holiness.

6. The purity by which the body became a temple of the Holy Ghost.

7. The purity which gave the power of healing the sick and of raising the dead; *i.e.*, the spirits of the dead!

8. They attained the mystic state of Elias, who was the Essenic Christ!

And in the middle of the Nineteenth Century, Bishop Lightfoot rises to explain that the Essenes were Fortune-tellers!

Orthodox Christianity knows nothing of Spiritualism to-day, and consequently can know nothing of Spiritualism in the past, because it is fact alone that can prove the fact. They reject it because it was repudiated by the founders of the historic faith; because it offers no facts to prove, whereas it does offer facts that furnish us with disproof of a physical resurrection. But it is absolutely necessary to be a phenomenal Spiritualist, or at least to know that phenomenal

Spiritualism is founded upon facts of possible human experience, before we can take the first step toward really understanding this matter of the beginnings, or gauge the impassable gulf of difference that lies between the Gnostic Religion and Historic Christianity. With the Gnostics knowledge was the foundation of their faith; but the Historic Christians made faith the basis of knowledge, and the first demand of the new faith was for the convert to believe that all the mythical typology of the past had been made literally true in the present. By faith the fable was crystallised into the dogma of historic fact.

The Gnostic doctrines of the pre-Historic religion were formulated as being those of knowledge, faith, and immortality. Knowledge was fundamental. On this their faith was founded by means of a first-hand acquaintanceship with those facts which gave them their faith for the present, and sustained it with something more than the hope or promise of continuity for the future. Knowledge, Faith, and Immortality! Historic Christianity was based upon faith without that knowledge, and those who knew the least were actually considered and designated the better believers, just as it is in the Salvation Army of to-day. Lord Bacon, in a most unworthy utterance, affirmed that "the more irrational and incredible any divine mystery is the greater the honour we do God in believing it, and so much the more noble is the victory of faith." Such, however, was the teaching of the Church whose divine mysteries were manufactured from misinterpreted mythology. Nor was it very difficult to literalise the mystical representation when a man like Origen could maintain that the planets were animated bodies and rational beings.

All the secrets of the great knowledge of the interior and mystical life, which M. Renan calls the "Most glorious creation of Christendom," were in possession of the Gnostics of various lands long ages earlier, whilst their *modus operandi* of ascertaining the truth was now to be rejected and denounced as damnable by the corporeal Christians, or carnalisers of the Christ. They not only let go, they anathematised the knowledge that was already won from nature, and prohibited the means of continuing it or of recovering it again.

The Gnostics, as Irenæus shows, pointed out the very serious error that was committed by those who imagined that the Christ had arisen in a mundane body, not knowing that "flesh and blood do not attain to the Kingdom of God!"

The Christ of the Gnostics was a mystical type continued from mythology to portray a spiritual reality of the interior life. Hence the Christ in this human phase could be female as well as male; Sophia as well as Jesus; the spirit of both sexes. It was impossible for such to become historical, or be made so, except by ignorantly mistaking a mythical Impersonation for a Hermaphrodite in Person!

What, for example, is the actual base of the "Great Renunciation" ascribed to the Buddha or the Christ in the doctrinal, mythical, or spiritual phase? It is this:--When the soul of man came to be considered as a divine principle of celestial origin, it was figured as being entirely opposed to the evil nature of matter; therefore, birth or manifestation in matter was a descent of the soul from the heaven of pristine condition into a lower state of impurity and impermanence; of disease, decay, and death, where it was bound to bear or struggle to get out of it again as soon as possible.

This soul, personified as the Divine Man in Buddha or the Christ is afterwards represented as being consciously able to renounce the pleasures of Paradise, and of its own free will and choice come down to earth as the Saviour of the World, by giving lessons in divinity and living a life so lowly that this life should be conquered by rejecting it on behalf of the other thus revealed to men! The mode of glorifying such a being is simply that of the infantile mind. The proof of his supernatural character is shown through his power of suspending the known laws of nature by miraculous means, such as are humanly impossible. As the Lord of Life he raises the dead! The tree bends down and bows its acknowledgment to him in the womb of his mother; or the wild beasts grow tame in presence of the radiant child that lights the darkness of the cave when born. As a mere babe he becomes a teacher to the teachers.

In youth he surpasses all competitors, conquers in every trial. All nature is turned into an elastic vesture that will fit this figure of the impossible--the *false* Ideal that makes our common everyday world a scene of phantasmal unrealities. In certain respects the Buddhist portrait of this divine Ideal, believed to have been realised in Gautama, transcends the Christian--in the depths of its tenderness, the range of its sympathies, and the embrace of its compassion. All true lovers of animals are naturally Buddhistic rather than Christian. For, it is upon the down-trodden beasts which perish that the Christian sets his foot for the first step upward as the possessor of an immortal soul. His brutalising belief, and baseless assumption, that animals have no souls, are guilty before God and responsible for most of the cruelties suffered by them throughout all Christendom today!

In his large love for the dumb things this Hindu Ideal Redeemer is greater, and stoops lower than the would-be Saviour of human beings alone, and only the Jewish part of them, who is portrayed as the Canonical Christ. But *cui bono?* when it is only an Ideal and that Ideal takes the place of possible reality. These false Ideals are forever fatal to human verity. What has the worship of Mary ever done for woman in the character of wife? You cannot live by a Lay figure. When once we know it to be unreal, whether as the Christ, or Buddha, or Madonna, it becomes a type that we cannot print from any longer, because it fails to impress deeply enough.

Whether considered as the God made human, or as man made divine, this character never existed as a person. That pre-historic Ideal Christ of the Gnosis had always personated the divine in human form, the Immortal incarnated, the Majesty within superior to all the physical conditions without, with power to bear and serve, to serenely suffer the ills of flesh, become a sacrifice and glory in the Cross of its earthly suffering.

Spiritual mediums were considered to be a kind of intermediate beings, because they first demonstrated the existence of a living link betwixt the divine mind and matter in the human form. But the original intermediate being was the spiritual nature itself, called the Son of God, the Christ within, which constituted that living link in whomsoever it existed. No human medium could become the Christ of the Gnosis, who represented a principle which could only become a person in a future state of being -- never in this world. So was it before the history alleged to have been lived, and so the fact remains today, and for ever. The historical was an impossible mode of realising that which could only be a spiritual possibility; and thus the truth according to the Gnosis has been refracted in the falsehood according to the History.

The Gnostic Christ was the real founder of Christianity! This was the Christ of the first Christians, and this was their model man, the Ideal meek and lowly one, which the writers of the Gospels have sought to realise in the form of historic personality. This lunar, solar, mystical, or spiritual type could not be made historical in the creed of those who knew, *i.e.*, the Gnostics. But it was humanized; it was turned into a one person, who became the one Christ in this world, and the one spirit of all others, for those who did not know. For the earliest appeal of the new faith was made to men who were so ignorant, according to the record, that when they had just witnessed a rising from the dead of certain historic characters, they did not comprehend what this rising again from the dead should mean!

Historic Christianity had retained possession of a dead Christ, the mere husk of the grub, together with a vague belief in the butterfly; and if you, likewise, believe in its one dead grub, you may cultivate the hope of some day, also, becoming a butterfly. But, for the Gnostics, the transformation from the chrysalis condition of matter to the spiritual was a natural fact of which they had an ever-present vitalising consciousness. They were transforming and seeking attainment all their life through; and their Christ was the representative type of that transformation of the mortal into an immortal.

Historic Christianity abolished the Gnostic spiritualism for all who accepted the false belief! Henceforth there was but one spirit, that of the historic Bringer of Immortality to Light; and, if any apparition appeared to the abnormal or normal vision, it would be the historic Christ for ever after! It was so with the vision of Paul, which was reported and perverted in the Book of Acts. When his inner eyes were opened he saw spirits--as Swedenborg and many others are reported to have done--whereupon they avowed he had seen the risen Jesus, their only witness for a spirit-world! So has it been with the non-Spiritualists ever since, for whom an apparition must be the Christ. In an island near Rotterdam, says Renan, the peasants believe that Christ comes to the bed of death to assure the elect of their justification. In point of fact many see him! On the other hand, the Buddhist "Lotus" declares that thousands of Buddhas show their faces to the virtuous man at the moment of his decease, which proves the Buddhas to be spirits. So has it been with the ecstatics and mediums in all the religious sects. Whenever they saw a spirit they saw Jesus the Christ their Saviour, because they knew of no other spirit or name--the history being established for the other world as well as in this--and so one delusion was bound to support the other; the true vision was made untrue; and all the facts of spiritualism have been falsified and turned into lying witnesses, to substantiate the truth of the Gospel history. All such manifestations as had previously occurred and had been attributed to the spirits of the departed, were now ascribed to the power of Christ, in whose name the prophesying was performed, the healing effected, and the mental medicine dispensed.

Henceforth there was to be no other name under heaven but this. In this name only were the Gentiles to have hope. Redemption was made dependent on this name; cripples were cured, the blind made to see, devils were cast out, the dead raised, sins remitted, souls saved, and eternal life ensured by belief on this name supposed to be New. At the mention of this name the dead arose up out of their graves, and, according to the testimony of Irenæus, they survived amongst the living many years! So much more potent was faith than fact. The earlier spiritualism was founded upon facts in nature, which did not need the desperate expedient of a miracle to explain. But in the later cult the more the miracle the larger loomed the supernatural, and the broader were the foundations for the belief that was based on faith instead of facts, and on Materialism plus Miracle.

They accounted for the spiritual phenomena of the Gnostics by declaring, as Justin Martyr did, that when the devil and the demons knew that Christ was believed on, and that he was expected "in every race," they put forth Simon, Menander, and the other Gnostics to deceive the multitude with magic. Because Spiritualism was naturally and for ever at war with the historical misinterpretation, Justin asserts that after the ascension of Christ into Heaven, the demons put forward certain men like Simon to declare that they were the Gods. Whereas, historic Christianity proclaimed them to be devils; and devils they have remained ever since, according to the false belief.

The founders of the Catholic Church were the

de-Spiritualizers of primitive Christianity, and the destroyers of the Gnostic religion as such, by placing their ban upon all Spiritualistic phenomena! The foundations of the ancient cult were to be built upon no longer.

In the recently discovered Didaché or the "Teaching of the Apostles," the facts of Spiritualism are admitted, and the practices of the prophets are recognized. They are spoken of as "ordering a table in the spirit," and of "assembling together for a Cosmic mystery." But those are the true mediums alone who have the "manners of the Lord;" and the law as laid down in these Didaché is:--"Thou shalt not play the mage! Thou shalt not practise witch-craft"--or spirit-intercourse. No prophet that speaks as one of the possessed is to be tried or tolerated. "Every sin shall be forgiven, but this sin shall not be forgiven."

It was now and henceforth to be Spiritualism without spirits, abstract and ideal, not tangible or real, an article of faith versus fact. We see from the Epistle of John how mortally afraid of Gnostic Spiritualism were the founders of the historical fraud. "Many deceivers are gone forth into the world that confess not that Jesus Christ cometh in the flesh." These words of John state the Gnostic position. Their Christ had not so come, and could not be carnalized. These Gnostics were in the world long before they heard of such a doctrine; but when they did they denied and opposed it. This, says John, is the anti-Christ. But, "every spirit which confesseth that Jesus Christ is come in the flesh is of God; and every spirit which annulleth Jesus is not of God. And this is the spirit of the anti-Christ whereof ye have heard that it cometh, and now it is in the world already."

A story is told of two early English saints, one of whom was supposed to have died. They were about to bury him, when, as he was being lowered into the grave, face upward and uncovered, he opened wide his ghostly staring eyes and told them he had only fallen into a trance. He had been into the other world, and found that what they were preaching about it in this was not true. There was no "Fall of Man," he said. "There is no hell," he cried; "no personal Christ--no Redeemer." But here his fellow-saint outside the grave interposed--"For God's sake fill in the earth and stop the blasphemer's mouth!" They did so, and the rest of his revelation remained unknown.

That was how the Catholic Christians dealt with the Gnostic Spiritualists when they had the power. They would shut up the living mouth of the Spirit-world, because the reports from the other side were fatal to the Historic fiction. They broke down the bridge between the two worlds, and proclaimed a great gulf fixed forever, which could only be crossed by faith in the Historic Jesus. Here the movement of Historic Christianity was a direct and deliberate shunting of the human mind from off the main line, the highway of its natural development, and running it head first into all sorts of bye-ways and blind alleys, from which we have had to turn back and grope out again as best we could for any progress to be made.

Historic Christianity originated with turning the Gnostic and Esoteric teachings inside out and externalising the mythical allegory in a personal human history. All that was interior with the knowers was made objective; all that was spiritual in significance was embodied to be made palpable for the ignorant. A corporeal Christ was substituted for the trans-corporeal man--a Christ whose advent was without, instead of the one that must be evolved within--a personal Saviour who died for all, instead of the Christ that was the living Spirit working within all. It was remarked by Augustine (de Civ. Dei, 7, 24) that the Gnostics "promised eternal life to anybody"--that is, with them the soul of man was an eternal principle, and the resurrection was not cunningly reserved for the elect who accepted the Historic belief.

The Gnostic claimed to be illuminated by the presence of the Christ within; the Christian, according to Justin, by the name of the Christ without. And a very curious mental link of connection between the genuine Gnostic and the counterfeit Historic Christ is apparent in the Ignatian Epistle to the Smyrneans. The writer says--"I know that even after his resurrection he was in the flesh, and I believe that he is so still." Now this combines both, after a fashion.

The writer is seeking to establish the history against those who denied that the Christ could be made a man. In doing this, he has recourse to the Gnostic Christ, who always was in the flesh, or matter, as the salt of soul, and the only spiritual Saviour from death and dissolution. Speaking from his Gnostic standpoint, Paul declared to the historic Christians who followed John and Peter, that God had sent them a working of error, that they should believe a lie, because they rejected the truth as it was according to his spiritual Gospel! The lie was established by externalising the Christ that can only dwell within -- by successfully falsifying for a time that truth which is true for ever. In this way, you see, that the coming of the Holy Spirit, which always had been within, was henceforth to be without. Thus, the descent of the Holy Ghost upon Jesus, in Jordan, is an external transaction. The Holy Spirit that comes from heaven in the form of a dove--a Gnostic type of the Spirit; that is, of both sexes--or, later on, as a whirlwind, in which the Gust and Ghost are one.

In the course of this conversion of the inner to the outer, we are told that the Holy Ghost, which always had been extant with the Gnostics, was not yet given, because the Historical Jesus was not yet glorified; but after he had risen from the grave, and returned bodily to the disciples, he breathed upon them, and said, "Receive ye the Holy Ghost." And again: the Holy Ghost, as an external effusion, could not be given until after forty days; whereas, in the Essenic Mysteries, the body of the disciple became the temple of the Holy Ghost when he had reached the sixth stage of interior progress. This shows the literalisers of the legend, the rationalisers of the mythos, the anti-mystics, the Exoterists, external-ising the Gnosis, and converting the matter of it into human history. There was to be neither Spirit within nor Spirit-world without for the ignorant Chris-tians, until the resurrection and ascension of Jesus had historically established both.

Two distinct charges are brought against the Carnalizers by Tatian in the second century. He cries out shame upon the Catholic Church, and exclaims, "You have given the Nazarite wine to drink, and commanded the prophets, saying, 'Prophesy not.'" They were debauching the Christian community and destroying the primitive Nazarite purity which Tertullian claimed for the Christians when he said, "We are they of whom it is written, 'Their Nazarites are whiter than snow.'" Next, they have determined to put an end to practical spiritualism on behalf of the new faith; and this is treated by Tatian as part of a subtle scheme for destroying the purity and spirituality of that Christianity which was primitive and non-historic, too!

The transformations of the Pagan cult into the Christian, and of the Gnostic into the historical representation, were effected behind the veil identifiable as the "Discipline of the Secret," the strictness of which was only relaxed after the fourth century, when the Truth had been hidden in a fog of falsehood; the inner mysteries turned to an outer mist, that made confusion cunningly complete.

The Gnostic Spiritualism was declared illegal and impious. The objective realities of the phenomenal Spiritualists, which had heretofore furnished the one bit of foothold in natural fact for a belief in the future life, were now discarded on behalf of the more subjective idealities derived from a faith that was founded by means of a fraudulent history mistranslated from a mystical fable.

The Roman Church adopted the Angels and Archangels of the Celestial Allegory as its Saints, including Saint Bacchus and Saint Satan in place of Guardian Spirits that were once human beings.

A dogma of the Real Presence of the Historic Christ was now substituted for the Real Presence of Spirit Friends in the earlier communion.

The mysteries in which the early Christian Neophytes had been initiated into a lawful communion with the dead were gradually suppressed; and in the sixth century we find the doctrine of a communion with the saints was substituted for the practical intercourse with spirits. It happens that the time when the doctrine was inserted in the Creed coincides almost exactly with the suppression of the mysteries which were connected with the so-called Agapæ of the early Christians! The Agapæ were only a continuation of the ancient Pagan funeral feasts and Eucharistic rites in honour of the departed. Hence they were held in the cemeteries and catacombs in presence of the dead, where the mummy-type or the Karest was the Christ, as the image of rising again; the image that was carried round and pointed to as a cause for festive rejoicing at the Egyptian feast! In this way we can watch the false faith taking the place of the facts.

And as the Gnostic sects and brotherhoods gave up the ghost, Historic Christianity assumed their glory. In this strange scene of transformation and dramatic illusion by some Satanic sleight of hand and turn of head, the afterglow of the ancient religions was changed into the dawn of the superseding faith, which was then proclaimed to be the fountain-head of all future enlightenment! or rather the waning light of ancient knowledge has been mistaken for the dawning of the New Belief; a dawn that was followed by the grey twilight that deepened into the thousand-years-long intellectual night of the Dark Ages.

It matters not what may be the relative share of responsibility attributable to knavery on the one hand and ignorance on the other, the fact remains that a huge and hideous mistake has been made, an irretrievable error committed in the name of Historic Christianity. For ages past the false faith did feed the flames of martyrdom with the fires of hell on pretext of giving light to them that it had covered with its smoke of torment and pall of darkness. And now the sun of a better day has arisen to put out the fires infernal, to disperse the clouds of human sighs, that have obscured the heavens so long, and to aid in drying the tears from our afflicted earth at last. Revelation, by means of Evolution, has now made known for ever that the fall of man was not historic fact. Humanity has not to bear the penalty eternally for a divine failure in the beginning of time.

This world is not a prison-house of fallen beings. Consequently, the promised redemption and proffered mode of salvation are a vain delusion, and all in vain has the spirit of the living Christ within been compelled to drag the dead body of the corporeal Christ from the grave for the purpose of proving the history for the ignorant, until its corruption is a sickening stench in the nostrils of the nations, and there is a clamour for the burial that shall get rid of both together. The history of Christ as our impersonated Saviour on earth, equally with the story of Adam's fall from Eden, is mythology misbelieved. The Old Testament was read backwards to be re-written as the New. The only original elements in this interpolation between the ancient Gnosis and modern science are those that prove false to the governing laws of the universe, and those facts of nature which make the sole true revelation.

Theory avails nothing in the presence of the fact that Historic Christianity was founded on the "Resurrection of the Flesh," and that it has left the world where it was itself, after putting out the Gnostic

Light, all in the dark concerning our spiritual continuity in death! Canon Gregory said only the other day if Jesus did not rise corporeally from the tomb, then that tomb must be the grave of Christianity. And the "Spectator" for August 13, 1887, speaking of the Greeks who died before the Resurrection was thus historically established, says:--"In the nature of things the Greeks could have had no sure hope of a glorious resurrection." Such was and is, when honestly confessed, the genuine Christian creed.

It does seem to me as if those arch-forgers in Rome had subtly succeeded in converting that which was true in the old religion into a secret support for all that was false in the new. Gnostic Christianity was absolutely, fundamentally, and for ever opposed to the historic rendering, and yet the Gnostic doctrines of the fourth Gospel, and of Paul's and James' Epistles, have been allowed to remain under cover and control as spiritual forces artfully tethered to draw for the physical and anti-Gnostic Faith. I am sometimes compelled to say to myself it has been most devilishly done!--and so have we!

We have Spiritualists to-day who lay hold of the Scriptures, or can be laid hold of, by means of the Gnosis that remains there as a lure, and turn it to the account intended, that is, as a decoy towards accepting the history. And so when the risen Christ reappears in the actual body that is missing from the grave, they are prepared to explain away the physical fact by means of the spiritual Gnosis. In that way nothing is bottomed, and nothing can be really understood; but, -- the purpose of the promoters, who were the founders of the falsehood, and who founded it well-nigh unfathomably, -- their purpose continues to be fulfilled.

In writing to a Christian spiritualist the other day, I said, "I know no better way of waging the battle for Truth than arraying the facts face to face on either side and letting them fight it out." His reply was, "I do not believe in your facts because I do not know." Now, that is good firm ground to stand upon, however late in life we take the position. But, to be of any real service, we must apply the same reason all round! As an adherent of Historic Christianity, that writer has all along been a Believer in what he did not know to be facts; and a believer just because he did not know; and now he finds it too late, perhaps, to correct his early belief by means of later knowledge! All I ask is that people shall no longer believe because they do not know.

No matter what they may call themselves--they are traitors to the Truth who will not face the facts or examine for themselves, but will go on repeating ignorantly, or in pious pigheadedness, the orthodox assumptions, and applying the hypotheses of accommodation to the Christian documents. You might as well expect to reach the next world by going round and round this, as to think of making ends meet by unifying the Gnostic religion with Historic Christianity. Phenomenal Spiritualists who go on philandering with the fallacies of the Christian faith, and want to make out that it is identical with Modern Spiritualism, have at last to face the great, indubitable fact that Historic Christianity was established as a non-Spiritualist and an anti-Spiritualistic religion! Its primary fact, its initial point of departure, its first bit of foothold for a new departure, was the acknowledgment of the physical resurrection of the dead Historic Christ. It is useless to try to wriggle out of that. The reappearance of the Corpus Christi is the fundamental fact of the Faith!

The strings are pulled so that the Marionette Messiah may be forced to exclaim that he is not a bodiless ghost; not a boneless phantom; not a spirit anyway; and he offers the proof palpable that he is none of your Spiritualistic or Gnostic Christs, or the spirit of anybody! Moreover, this is the veritable dead body that is missing from the tomb! And still further, the passage in Luke has been altered from Marcion's "Gospel of the Lord" on purpose to substitute the Corporeal Christ of Historic Christianity for the Spiritual representation of the Gnostics. In Marcion's version the word *phantasma* is used, and this has not only been omitted by Luke; the phantom is made to protest very emphatically that he is not in anywise phantasmal, but is a being of flesh and blood even as they are; and after demonstrating the fact, clinches it by asking if they have got anything there for him to eat! The entire fabric of the new faith rested upon the reality of a physical resurrection; and it is too late now to shift the basis of the edifice by trying to lift it bodily, like the city of Chicago, on to the higher and surer ground of Spiritualism, so as to find a firmer basis for it and all its weight of errors!

We can trace the very bifurcation and fresh starting-point of the new faith in the account given of the resurrection in the Canonical Gospels. They proclaimed the resurrection of the dead in Jesus and through him only! The historic Jesus who alone had power to open the gateways of the grave, and who had personally left with Peter the keys that lock up heaven and open hell. There was nothing to constitute a new faith in a spiritual resurrection. That was already the common property of the Gnostics, whether called Pagans or Christians. That was according to the natural fact, and here only was the miracle, in the dead body rising again to prove the presence and the power of the divinity. Such is the religious foundation, for which the Christians are responsible Trustees!

As a Spiritualist, then, I assert that the new Christian dispensation was founded upon the death and burial of the ancient spiritualism; or upon the gagging of it and getting it underground dead or alive! And the tomb out of which a corporeal Christ was believed to have emerged as the Saviour of the World, and brought immortality to light by a physical resurrection from the dead, has been the burial-place of genuine Spiritualism for 1800 years. For this reason the defenders of the faith were bound to make war upon the facts of phenomenal spiritualism, and persecute and put the psychical demonstrators to death, which they did with a consuming fury so long as they were allowed.

The terrible craze that was caused by this perversion of the ancient wisdom has sown the germs of insanity broadcast, and half-filled the world with pious lunatics for whom it offers no cure, and who are still told to look forward for an asylum in the world to come. But such pernicious teaching will make people as insane for another life as for this! Here, or hereafter, falsehood must be fraudulent, though it may be found out too late! What of the myriads of suffering souls who have been forced to wear the blinkers of ignorance all through this life for fear they should learn to see for themselves--who were drugged and deceived from birth till death with the nostrums of a false deluding faith. What of them when they awake from their stupor in death to find out that they have been foully, cruelly hocussed with a creed that was an illusion for this life and a delusion for the next.

> *Delusion that is perfectly complete*
> *For those who die to find out the deceit!*

If the teachers of the fleshly cult could but see *how* their fallacies dissolve in death--how the false ideal set up in this life dislimns and fades as the terrible light of reality whitens in the next; if they could but see that mournful multitude of the help-lessly deceived who staked their all upon the truth of what they had been taught and find they have lost because the teaching was false! If you could see them wander up and down on the other side of the dark river and wring their hands over their blighted hopes and broken hearts; hear the pitiful wailings for the Christ that is no more objective there than he was here--for the visionary glory that they may not grasp, the distant rainbows, never reached, that weep themselves away in tears--for the lifeboat gone to wreck on the wrong shore because of the false beacon-lights.

If you could only dream how these poor souls desire to have the deception made known on this side of life--how they want to send some word of warning to their friends--how they will almost hiss at me through the mouths of mediums whenever they have the chance, as if their fierce feelings had turned into tongues of flame, praying for us to work on faster and cry louder against the established lie, for time is getting short and the helpers are few, and the atmosphere around each live soul is so deathly dense with indifference! This would be unbearable but for those calm other voices of the Gnostics who in this life walked our world lords of themselves with "inward glory crowned," and who lived on after the Gnosis was suppressed and the ancient oracles made dumb--who live on yet, and are working with us still--who fill and inflate us at times with their influence, as if each single soul of us were a hundred thousand (*"cent mille,"* as his men used to call Napoleon). It is they who are joining hands with us to-day to bridge over that dark gulf betwixt two worlds which the historic and fleshly faith first excavated, and has been deepening and widening now for eighteen centuries.

This is the Resurrection Day of the pre-Christian

Gnosticism, as shown by the recent revival of Spiritualism, by the restoration of the Tree of Knowledge, by the elevation of Womankind, instead of the Fall of man; and we are living witnesses of the fact that

> *"Truth, crushed to earth, shall rise again,*
> *The eternal years of God are hers;*
> *But Error, wounded, writhes with pain,*
> *And dies among his worshippers!"*

NOTE

❧

I have been asked whether I am able to explain by means of the Egyptian Mythos, the two diverse statements in the Gospel according to Luke and the Book of Acts concerning the ascension of Jesus into Heaven. In Luke the risen Christ is "carried up into Heaven" on the third day following the crucifixion. In the Acts he is not "taken up" into Heaven until the fortieth day, or after forty days! Such serious discrepancies as these are forever irreconcilable as history, but they are found to contain the very facts that reconstitute the Mythos.

The resurrection of Osiris at the Autumn equinox was lunar; at the vernal equinox it was solar. After he was betrayed to his death, when the sun was in the sign of Scorpio, he rose again on the third day as Lord of Light in the moon, or as Horus, the child of the mother-moon. The solar resurrection was at the vernal equinox when the sun entered the first of the upper signs and Orion rose. This time it was in the character of the second Horus, the adult of 30 years; and this second resurrection followed the forty days of mourning for the suffering God which were celebrated in the Mysteries, and survive in a Christianized form as our Lent. And just as the myth of the double Horus in the two characters of the child of 12 years, and the adult Horus of 30 years, has been continued in the Gospels to furnish the two phases in the life of Jesus, so have the two different resurrections with their correct dates been applied to the Christ made historical.

Thus interpreted by means of the Mythos these two versions of one alleged fact tend to corroborate my explanation already made that the two different dates for the crucifixion given in the otherwise irreconcilable accounts belong to the luni-solar reckoning in the same luni-solar myth. In Egyptian the signs of a half- moon and fourteen days are identical; and in the dark half of the moon Osiris was torn into fourteen parts. Therefore the 14th of the lunar month was the day of full moon. Whereas in the soli-lunar month of thirty days the 15th was the middle of the month. Now the crucifixion or the crossing at Easter was and still is determined by the day of full moon. This will be on the 14th of the month of twenty-eight days in the reckoning by the moon only, but on the 15th of the month according to the soli-lunar reckoning. The 14th of the month would be the lunar reckoning of Anup = John, and the 15th that of Taht-Mati = Mathew in the two forms of the Egyptian Mythos. Both reckonings were extant in two different cults and both were separately continued by the Eastern and Western Churches for the one day of the crucifixion.

Both cannot be historically correct, but they are both astronomically true. Both could be made to meet at a given point in the total combination which was determined by the conjunction of the sun and moon at the equinox as *the* day of full moon. But the two different dates for the mid-month remained, and these are represented by the traditions of two different dates for the crucifixion. Both the lunar and the solar dates could be utilised by the Mythos, in which there were two crucifixions and two resurrections, though these will bear witness for the single fact of the historical crucifixion. As we have seen, the two ascensions of Osiris on the third day and at the end of forty days, have been preserved, and are repeated as historical transactions. Two different Crosses were also contained in the Christian Iconography as the cross of Autumn and of

Easter; and although we may not be able to show two crucifixions in the Canonical Gospels, nevertheless the total matter of the Mythos is there. When Jesus was led up into the wilderness to be tempted of the devil, and to suffer during forty days, we have the parallel to the struggle between Osiris and Sut, which was celebrated during the forty days of mourning in the mysteries.

Moreover, there were two days of death or crucifixion kept in Rome until the present century, when the dead Christ used to be laid out and exhibited on the Thursday before Good Friday; and two days of resurrection were also celebrated in the two Sabbaths on Saturday and Sunday. As the Apostolic Constitutions show, both of these days were continued for the two weekly holidays of the Christians, Saturday being the day of rising again on the 7th day of the week in the lunar cult; Sunday, the Sabbath of the 8th day, according to the solar resurrection. Such are the fundamental facts; and, to my thinking, they are of sufficient force to cleave the Canonical history right in two, each half being then claimed by the Mythos. Here, as elsewhere, the Mythos does explain the fact, but only by abolishing the history. From beginning to end the ascertainable facts are astronomical, and interpretable solely by means of the Gnostic explanation of the Egyptian

Mythos, which always denied, because it disproved, the alleged human history.

The same correspondent desires to know whether I would exclude the Bible from our children's schools. Most certainly. I would have the Bible-basis superseded for all future teaching as unscientific, immoral, and false to the facts in nature. The mass of people who are Bible-taught never get free from the erroneous impressions stamped on their minds in their infancy, so that their manhood or womanhood can have no intellectual fulfilment, and millions of them only attain mentally to a sort of second childhood.

Copyright

Also Available

www.ingramcontent.com/pod-product-compliance
Lightning Source LLC
Chambersburg PA
CBHW012013110726
47993CB00008B/3041